Economic
Development
in
Perspective

ECONOMIC
DEVELOPMENT
IN
PERSPECTIVE

John Kenneth Galbraith
UNITED STATES AMBASSADOR TO INDIA

1962

HARVARD
UNIVERSITY
PRESS

Cambridge

At the request of the author,
the royalties earned on sales of this volume
are to be devoted to educational purposes.

Preface

THIS small book is an outgrowth of five lectures which I gave in five major Indian educational communities—the University of Madras, the University of Calcutta, the University of Bombay, the University of Rajasthan, and the Indian Institute of Public Administration in New Delhi—in the summer and autumn of 1961. In recent years the literature of economic development has become very extensive and its language very complex. Under such circumstances there is always danger of losing sight of essentials. In the enthusiasm of the discussion of interesting details we confuse a part of the problem with the whole. The lectures were, as the title indicates, an attempt to put the development task into clear and simple perspective. Perhaps I should say that this was the task of the four of the five lectures; the fifth is a little more specialized, for it is concerned with the important problem of how one employs the principal instrument of industrial development, namely the corporation.

When these lectures aroused some interest, not only in India but elsewhere, I was persuaded without great difficulty to rearrange them in this form. I hope that they make some small contribution to the understanding of what, without question, is the most important and humane task on which men are now engaged. I do not suppose that everything here will encounter the agreement of all who read this book. It may be of some comfort that their disagreement is with me. In this age of organization there are some things which remain within the exclusive competence and jurisdiction of individuals. Discussion of the kind contained herein would seem to be an example.

J. K. G.

Contents

Economic
Development
in
Perspective

I

Economic Development in Perspective

IN the years since World War II, in all parts of the literate world, we have had an exceedingly active discussion of economic development. Although one should always be wary of comparisons, this discussion can be compared in vigor with that which got under way after the publication of Smith's inquiry into *The Nature and Causes of the Wealth of Nations* in 1776 and to which in the following sixty or seventy years Bentham, Malthus, and John Stuart Mill, among others, made their notable contributions. The occasion is the same. At present, as then, nations are in the beginning stages of national development. The new countries of Asia and Africa are now concerned, as were those of Western Europe in the late eighteenth and early nineteenth centuries, to understand the processes on which progress depends. In these last years scholars in the economically more advanced countries have joined, and on occasion have led, the discussion. Americans can be more than a little proud of the intensity of the interest in the economics of development in these last years in the United States.

Both in the new states and in the old states it has been recognized that economic development is an imperative. Indeed, this has been a distinguishing feature of the recent as compared with the earlier discussion. At least until the time of Marx, the problem of economic progress was explored with a measure of philosophical detachment. In the years since World War II it has been characterized by a note of high urgency. The nineteenth century discussion was in a world that was rather proud of what was happening. The twentieth century discussion is in a world which feels that a great deal more must happen and very soon.

The recent discussion of development has also differed from the earlier in being remarkably more sophisticated. We now have growth models —hypotheses as to the nature of the process of economic growth—some of considerable mathematical refinement and a few that are wholly incomprehensible. Capital-output ratios and

marginal capital-output ratios are now calculated
more or less on a mass production basis for the
various components of five-, seven-, and ten-year
plans and for perspective plans beyond. Missions
pass through the underdeveloped countries avoid-
ing each other only by adhering to closely planned
schedules and accumulating new information or
joyously rediscovering the already known. There
is now a considerable sociology and a sizable
anthropology of backwardness. We are told that
Mill by the age of seven was master of the Greek
classics. Were he now to reappear some ninety
years after his death he might well decide, after
seeing how intricate are the matters on which
he once wrote, to stay with Plato and Xenophon.

Yet it would be a mistake to identify complexity with completeness and sophistication
with wisdom. There are some serious shortcomings in the modern discussion. And these
become evident as we compare it with the earlier
debate.

· 2 ·

It is our pride that the recent discussion of
development has been scientific—that terms and
concepts have been rigorously defined and so
employed that scholars working on different

aspects of the problem can communicate with each other with some certainty, can correct each other as necessary, and each by adding his piece of knowledge to the common stock can thus add to the total wisdom. The earlier discussion was less precise but more grand. Smith, Malthus, Bentham, and Marx were builders of systems; they concerned themselves with the aggregate requirement of progress. The principles of good government, the inducements to individual performance, the role of popular enlightenment, the foundations of thrift, the effect of competition and of monopoly, the relation between social classes, the reasons why some people, notably the English, worked hard and others, notably the Irish, worked less hard, were all grist for their highly diversified mill. Indeed, anything that was deemed to have a bearing on economic advance was considered. The only test was broad relevance to the questions: What made for economic progress? Or, on the other hand, what led to stagnation—to the much-discussed stationary state?

The nineteenth century debate was conducted by a rather small number of men. By its nature it was confined to those who could grasp and articulate the great issues. Only great men could thus participate—we have often heard it said that each generation produces but one philosopher. The modern discussion, fortunately for those of us who essay to speak, has been much more democratic. That is because it has been concerned with the parts of the problem rather than the whole. Men with a usefully cosmic view of society are scarce. Many can contribute to knowledge of bits and pieces. It may not be easy to elucidate the relation of a philosophical or religious idea to economic change. But almost anyone can come up with some useful ideas on the priority to be attributed to machine tools in the next Five-Year Plan.

Here, it seems to me, lie the weakness and even the dangers of the current discussion of economic development. We have been enthusiastically and quite capably discussing the parts of the problem; we have paused all too infrequently to inquire whether they fit into a viable whole. We have looked at the things which contribute to economic development; we have given too little attention to inquiring whether they are being employed in a context that is favorable to development. As a result we have probably wasted a good deal of time and effort doing things which were right in themselves but which made little or no contribution to progress because they were done in an environment which was inconsistent with advance. The environment has not been examined. It has somehow been assumed to be favorable to development.

· 3 ·

Let me be more specific. In the years since World War II, in the absence of any over-all consideration of the conditions of economic advance of the kind that was offered a century earlier, we have made two assumptions. They are:

(1) That the world is divided between developed and underdeveloped countries. In the developed countries economic progress is more or less automatic—or in any case it is easily within the powers of the country itself if it follows an intelligent economic policy. Development is possible in any underdeveloped country. It requires the provision of certain missing components.

(2) These missing elements, on the identity of which there is a good deal of agreement, are modern technical knowledge or know-how, capital, specially trained manpower, and a sound plan for using capital, manpower, and technical knowledge. If these are provided there will be progress.

The standard prescription for economic development proceeds directly from this diagnosis. Technical assistance is obtained from abroad. Steps are taken to increase the supply of domestic savings and of capital from both domestic and foreign sources. Men are sent abroad for training. A five-year or seven-year or ten-year plan is devised.

This action will indeed be sound if the diagnosis of the development problem is sound. If that diagnosis is unsound we will be having a good deal of waste motion in the world. It is my unhappy feeling that the diagnosis leaves a great deal to be desired. That it is more nearly valid for India than for most other countries can be of only limited comfort even in India, for the task of overcoming poverty and privation is one that lies on the conscience of all mankind. Let us look more at the present diagnosis in the context of some practical cases.

· 4 ·

We have said that capital and technical knowledge are the missing elements. But in many of the newer African states national government is still in its beginning stages, and in parts of Latin America it has never been brought to a minimal level of efficiency. Under these circumstances investment, whether public or private, is subject to the risks, uncertainties, and eccentricities of poor public administration. It is idle to imagine that good development plans can be created or carried out without a good government to do it. And neither technical assistance nor trained technicians do well, or are even much needed, where administration is indifferent or bad. The best agricultural scientist cannot make much headway as adviser to a nonexistent ministry. The finest tax authority goes to waste if the minister does not believe in collecting taxes, does not want to do so, or has an overly developed feeling for his friends. The first task here is not to get capital or technicians but to build competent organs of public administration.

In the last century nothing occupied a more prominent place among the requirements for economic and social advance than public education and popular enlightenment. In the new states today, or the older ones without developed systems of popular education, one also wonders if schoolbooks should not come before machine tools. Popular education releases the energies not of the few but of the many. And it opens the way to technical knowledge. Literate people will see the need for getting machines. It is not so clear that machines will see the need for getting literate people. So under some circumstances at least popular education will have a priority over the dams, factories, and other furniture of capital development.

Finally, in many countries any serious look at the larger system must soon come to focus on the shortcomings of the social order—on arrangements under which wealth and political power are a monopoly of a small minority of the population and the masses, accordingly, are excluded from all incentives to improvement. Even the most eloquent agricultural extension expert cannot explain the advantage of growing two grains of wheat where but one flourished before if the peasant knows full well that both will go inevitably to his landlord. The best-considered forms of agricultural investment or the most sophisticated techniques of agricultural extension are worthless if the cultivator knows out of the experience of the ages that none of the gains will accrue to him.

In short, on even the most preliminary view of the problem, effective government, education, and social justice emerge as critically important. In many countries, in diagnosing the barriers to advance, it is lack of these that is of critical importance. And it follows that until these barriers are removed little will come from capital investment and technical assistance. While plans may be big on paper they will be small in result.

· 5 ·

I have said that the present diagnosis of the causes of underdevelopment, with its stress on capital, technical assistance, and planning, does not fit a country such as India too badly. India has an effective government; there is a substantial measure of literacy; she has a backlog of administrative and entrepreneurial talent; there is a solid commitment to the goals of social justice and social progress. At the same time the propensity to consume is high and the rate of saving is low, and the problem of capital supply is especially serious for that part which must be obtained from abroad. Under these circumstances attention has naturally been focused on the question of financial support to investment.

We have here an important reason for our misapprehension of the problem of development. India is by far the largest and most populous of the underdeveloped countries, China apart. Her development has attracted more attention than that of any other country partly because she has the most competent planners and the most articulate journalists and professors. India also has, despite their shortcomings, the best statistics, and, as all economists know, it is difficult to mount much of a discussion of development of a country where even imaginary gross national product data are unavailable. As a result the world has come, in far greater degree than has been realized, to identify development as a whole with the experience of India, or, more accurately, India and Pakistan. Since capital and technically trained manpower are the limiting factors in these lands they are assumed to be the limiting factor everywhere. Since competent planning is possible in India and Pakistan it is assumed to be possible everywhere.

The United States has also been responsible for some of the overemphasis on capital and technical know-how and talent. As a nation we have a healthy respect for money and its uses. And in the United States economic accomplishment depends not on the changing will of the government, not on winning the right social climate, not on finding literate workers, for these are available and assumed. Accomplishment depends on finding the capital and recruiting the engineers, scientists, and technicians. The world, in short, has generalized from the experience of the Asian subcontinent and we have generalized from our own. Those who praise cooperation in these matters should observe that it extends even to misleading students of economic development.

· 6 ·

What is the lesson? It is not that capital or technical assistance or technical training are unimportant or that planning is a waste of time. India, where these are vitally important, is competent proof to the contrary. The lesson is that we can no longer have one diagnosis of the causes of underdevelopment. Rather we must have the particular diagnosis which fits the particular country. And in few cases will the causes of backwardness or the requirements of progress be quite the same.

More specifically we must recognize that economic development is a process*—one that extends in range from new nations of Africa but slightly removed from their tribal structure to the elaborate economic and social apparatus of Western nations. At each stage along this con-

* Although his stages inevitably invite debate, Professor Rostow's signal contribution has been in moving consideration of the problem of development dramatically in this direction. (*The Stages of Economic Growth*, Cambridge, 1960.)

tinuum there is an appropriate policy for further advance. What is appropriate at one stage is wrong at another.

In the early stages it undoubtedly involves the building of organs of public administration and the provision of an educated minority, a nucleus of people who can build the system of public administration and, for that matter, everything else. Then comes the task of popular enlightenment. This enables the masses of the people to participate in economic activity. And it opens men's minds, as they can be opened in no other way, to new methods and new techniques. Apart from its cultural role, popular literacy is a highly efficient thing. Needless to say, it is also the mainspring of popular aspiration. As such it adds strongly to the desire for development.

If development is to depend on popular participation, then there must be a system of popular rewards. There can be no effective advance if the masses of the people do not participate; man is not so constituted that he will bend his best energies for the enrichment of someone else. As literacy is economically efficient, so is social justice.

As one proceeds along the line, other requirements enter, and, depending on population and resource endowment, these will be different in different countries. Capital becomes the touch-stone of development, the limiting factor, only in countries that are well along the line. Indeed, there is a distinct possibility that capital provided to countries in the earliest stages of development will be wasted. Only in a relatively sophisticated stage of development can it be well and wisely used in any considerable quantity.

At the last stop along this line are the so-called developed countries. In these—the United States, the United Kingdom, the USSR, Germany, France—capital ceases to be the limiting factor. Development becomes dependent on a complex of forces—scientific and technical skills and imagination, quality of working force, ability to make full use of available resources, clarity of national goals—which need not concern us here.

To see the process of development as a line along which the nations of the world are spaced, in their various stages of development, is to see both the process of and the policy for development with considerably enhanced clarity.

Thus it goes without saying that we can no longer speak of a common prescription for development. Any effort to offer such a general formula will be productive only of waste, frustration, and disappointment. And so, likewise, will be generalization from the experience of a country in one stage of development to the needs of a country in another stage. To generalize from the experience of the United States to the needs of India will be productive of error, but so, equally, will generalization from the case of India to that of Dahomey or Chad.

Instead, the need is for a plan appropriate to the particular stage in each country. In the early stages the development plans will not be very elaborate or complex; they will be concerned with the first essentials of administrative structure and with education and social reconstruction. In these early stages, also, development encounters the appalling problems of the closed circle. How does a country without effective organs of public administration develop them, since bad government is not self-correcting but self-perpetuating? How does a country without an educated elite create one, since to extend education takes educated people? How bring about social reform when the class structure places political power in the hands of those who are likely to resist it? These are intensely difficult questions, although perhaps not quite as difficult as they sound. Other countries have broken out of the circle. And the drive for development, in

Other countries have certainly broken out eg. Sierra Leone where there is a high level of illiterates who just cast their votes for a Le 1 or 2.

our day, is a force of great independent power, and it is not kind to those who, in defense of vested interest, stand in its way. In any case those who are concerned with development will not remove these obstacles by pretending they do not exist.

As I have said, in countries that have conquered these first problems, capital and technical knowledge become the limiting factors. India's present need for capital is based not on a low level of development. It is the result, as compared with the other new nations, of a relatively high level of development that enables her to use capital effectively. It is only at this stage, where consideration must be given to how scarce investment funds can be most effectively used and where different uses of capital must be horizontally integrated and phased over time, that planning becomes very complex. We could make no more serious mistake than to imagine that the kind of planning that is done by India or Pakistan is essential for nations in all stages of development. In earlier stages it is neither necessary nor possible.

II

The Developing and the Developed

DEVELOPING countries, I have suggested, can be thought of rather as beads being moved along a string. There was considerable advantage in being one of the countries that was first along that line. The nations that led the way—Britain, France, the United States—could take their achievements at their face value. Whatever they accomplished could be regarded with satisfaction. None did better. Exuberant pride in accomplishment was the mood of nineteenth century Britain. It is still in a considerable measure the mood of twentieth century America. The countries that came late, by contrast, have high and difficult standards not of their own making. They are faced always with comparisons —comparisons with the American or Soviet productive plant, comparisons with American or British living standards.

There is another troublesome matter. In a very poor arrangement of human affairs, development becomes easier the farther it proceeds. That is because each step in this process invariably makes the next one easier. Given no competent organs of public administration it is hard to develop any. But given a few good men training others they can soon be extended. Given no teachers it is hard to launch an educational system. Given a few teachers they too can train others, and given many teachers the training process becomes easy and almost automatic. Saving and capital accumulation are exceedingly painful in a poor country where the pressure of current need is very great. In a more affluent community saving is much easier. In a rich country savings may, of course, be excessive.

The consequence of this arrangement is that the more developed countries are constantly widening their advantage over those that follow behind. On occasion they blame those that follow for their poor performance. And to those that follow, progress must often seem disappointing. It would be well were we all to realize that if the pace of less favorably situated countries is slow it is not necessarily because their efforts are less. Most likely it is because their task is so much greater.

· 2 ·

To see the countries of the world not as divided between the developed and the underdeveloped but as spaced along a line representing
various stages of development is essential for ob-
taining an accurate view of the problem of assistance. For when development is so regarded we
see that no group of countries is uniquely quali-
fied to extend assistance and no other group is
similarly condemned to the role of recipients.
Rather each country has something to gain from
those that are in front. And it has something to
offer those that follow. The provision of aid is
seen, as it should be seen, as a cooperative
endeavor in which all countries may participate.

And while there will be differences in what is
given and what is received as we pass along the
line, I am not sure that the contribution of the
less developed countries is necessarily less. For
the more developed countries the provision of
capital is an obvious form of assistance. But as
countries such as India work out their problems
of popular education, family planning, and land
consolidation this experience will be exceedingly
valuable to those that follow along the line. I
venture to think that India can be a better

teacher here than the United States. She has
been much closer to the practical problem.

But let me rather stress the principle. To
divide the world as between the aiding and the
aided is both wrong and psychologically damaging. Development is a task in which many
need help and as many have something to offer.
This, henceforth, is how we must regard the
task.

· 3 ·

Now let me say a more specific word about
borrowing and lending of resources and experience between countries in different positions
along the development line. Given the different
stages of development, nothing is more natural
than that countries should look for guidance to
the experience of those that have gone before.
And nothing is more desirable than that those
who have gone first should make both experience
and tangible assistance available to those who
come later. In the years since World War II
such borrowing and lending of experience and
resources has become a commonplace. It is a
matter on which the United States has taken a
considerable lead. It will, I have always thought,
be our best remembered contribution to the
comity of nations.

Borrowing and lending between countries differently positioned along the development line is, however, a matter which calls for great judgment and great discrimination. The wrong things as well as the right things can be given or received. The experience of others can be wisely adapted and great good can come from it. And the practice of others can be unwisely adopted so as to do positive harm. Despite these difficulties and dangers much of the borrowing and lending, especially of experience, that has gone on between developing countries since World War II has been exceedingly casual, as though no problem were involved. Again let me specify.

There are three things which are possessed by the more advanced country which can be borrowed by those following it along the line. They are: (1) capital; (2) technology; (3) organization. The transmission of each of these between countries in different stages of development involves both rewards and dangers.

It is hard at first glance to imagine any of the less developed lands' being damaged by an excess of capital. And, as I have noted, countries in the higher stages of development accumulate capital far more easily than those in the less advanced stages. This is one reason why lending between advanced and less advanced countries on concessional terms—at low or zero rates of interest and for long terms of repayment—should be considered normal and natural. No one should be excessively impressed by economic aid which is in the form of ten-year loans at 6½ per cent. Few countries in any early stage of development can safely pay the price of purely commercial credits.

But even loans at low or zero rates, or forthright grants of capital, have their dangers. The ability to use capital in any considerable volume is itself the result of development. If it is available before the conditions for its use are available it will be ineffectively employed or possibly wasted. The provision of power and transportation to trained, literate, and socially emancipated people is bound to be productive. The productivity is far less certain if these things are provided to people who are still enslaved by ignorance or a backward social system.

Even in a country such as India which has reached the stage where it can use capital in quantity there are dangers. Borrowing from abroad can be a substitute for earning from abroad. Earnings depend on efficient and low-cost production that takes advantage of the tendency for nations in the more advanced stages to become what Keynes once called "high-cost, high-living" countries. Any friend of India must view with some concern the rather uninspiring behavior of Indian exports in the last five years. At a roughly similar stage in her industrialization, Japan had no alternative but to force her products onto the markets of the world. This was not a formula which made for universal popularity. But it did provide the earnings for investment which insured her further growth. It is doubtful if aid, however generous, can ever be a substitute for such earnings and for the independence and self-confidence that they afford.

· 4 ·

The borrowing of technology is also a subtle matter. In principle it is highly desirable. One advantage of being second in line is that the country so placed can take advantage of what has been worked out, often with great labor and cost, by those who have gone before. One must know, however, why the thing was worked out. Was it a step forward in a process or product of universal application? Or was it an adaptation to the requirements of advanced economic development itself? High-yielding maize hybrids, the Japanese method of rice cultivation, improved fertilizer use, the L-D process of steel production, are advances of general application. They economize all resources. They are as appropriate and important for the less as for the more developed country. But much of the technology of the more advanced countries represents an accommodation to labor shortages or reflects the other special requirements of the more advanced economy. The mechanical cotton picker and the modern heavy farm tractor are innovations of this sort. Their use on the farms in the United States reflects the fact that labor for hire is exceedingly scarce. This technology should not be taken over by countries in the earlier stages of development. To do so is to waste scarce resources and handicap development and, much more than incidentally, to add to unemployment.

Thus it is a mark of wise development planning to copy from the countries in the more advanced stages. And it is also a mark of wise planning not to do so. The distinction which I have just made between innovations of universal application and those which are merely adaptations to higher stages of development is not an easy one to apply. But it is more likely to be applied if the need for the distinction is at least recognized. Not long ago, in a neighboring Asian country where there is much unemployment and where wages are low, I saw expensive automatic gates imported from abroad being installed at the railroad crossing. These are a necessary development in those countries where no one is any longer available for the reflective life of the railway gateman. But not here. Had the distinction I am making been more clearly in mind considerable money would have been saved and the gatemen would have remained gratefully at their posts.

Where imitation is appropriate, it should be unabashed and unashamed. This will not be applauded by the more advanced countries; they have often felt that such behavior by the newcomer is not quite sporting. The British in the last century spoke most disrespectfully of the imitative tendencies of the Germans; no sooner did Sheffield have something that was good than Solingen had the same thing in a cheaper model. More recently the Japanese and the Soviets have been similarly criticized. Those who come later should be undeterred. They should take unblushing advantage of the paths that were broken by those who went first. The advantages

of late arrival are all too few. Those that exist
should be exploited.

· 5 ·

So much for borrowing capital and technology. I come now to borrowing of organization, a term I use broadly to include government
and its services, and educational, welfare, and
economic organization. Here, in my view, the
dangers are greatest of all. Such borrowing is
now very casual. Because a particular organization or service—a government department, educational institution, or agricultural or industrial
service—exists in a more advanced country it is
imagined that it makes an important contribution to development. Therefore it should be
recreated in the countries that are in the less
advanced stages. It will aid their development
too.

This line of reasoning, if such it may be
called, is a rich source of error. Often, and I
think usually, the organization and services of
the more advanced country are not the cause of
its development but the result. They reflect an
accommodation to the needs of more advanced
development or they are made possible by that
level of development. Injudicious and ill-con-

sidered borrowing and lending of such organization will not help development but will hinder
it. The Government of India is a complex and
multifarious thing which reflects the great vari-
ety of tasks undertaken by India in her stage of
development. An equally complex organization
would be a major misfortune for one of the
newer African states with, for the foreseeable
future, a far simpler range of tasks. A great many
features of the governmental, educational, agricultural, and industrial organization of the
United States are not important for American
development. They exist because a relatively advanced stage of development makes them necessary or, on occasion, because we can afford the
unimportant. Their transfer to India is equally
disastrous. If luxuries of the educational curriculum, esoteric educational institutions, refined
agricultural services, and a wide range of public
services are adopted before their time they will
draw resources and energies from the tasks that
are strategically vital for development. This is
not beneficial; it is harmful. Let me press the
point.

A hundred years ago the development of the
trans-Mississippi plains in the United States
called above all else for a land policy which

would get the land settled and plowed and a transportation system which would get the products to market. To this end the government surveyed the land, gave 160 acres to anyone who had proved his good intentions by farming it for a few months, and subsidized the building of railways. These essentials being provided, development proceeded with unexampled speed. It was our unquestioned good fortune that community education experts, grain marketing analysts, home advisers, vocational counselors, communciations specialists, or public safety counselors had not been invented. Had these existed, attention would have been drawn from the strategically central tasks of getting the farms settled and the railways built. And they would have been a burden on the backs of people who could ill afford such luxuries.

Today in the United States these more elaborate services can easily be afforded. And in the present stage of our development they may be needed. Transferred to Africa, or to India, they may be as redundant and even damaging as they would have been in the United States in its comparable stage of economic development.

The burden of proof must be on those who propose the transfer of organization and services. It is a far more delicate business than we have imagined. This is a warning to those of us who have been lenders just as much as to those who have been borrowers and perhaps more.

· 6 ·

I have dwelt on what I believe to be important misconceptions of the development problem when viewed from the perspective of different nations—misconceptions which experience now allows us to correct. We should not be surprised that there have been errors. To mount a major attack on privation and backwardness is an enormously complex task. It was necessary that we simplify; and it was inevitable, perhaps, that oversimplification would lead to mistakes. It would have been a far greater error to postpone action and await a perfect view of the problem. For we would not be wiser now had we not learned from the experience of these past years. And experience is a considerable teacher, even though, as Oscar Wilde once observed, it is also the name we give to our mistakes.

III

On the Theory of
Development Planning

Few words in our time are more fashionable in economic and political discussion than "planning," or are used, one imagines, with less precision. This absence of precision was perhaps most admirably illustrated in the early forties by the eminent British soldier and philosopher, Colonel Blimp, who, on taking note of the current concern for postwar economic prospects, was heard to say: "All this planning, it can lead only to chaos. But one thing you can say for chaos; it gives real scope for free enterprise."

This imprecision was long matched by the emotions which the word "planning" aroused. For some planning was the *sine qua non* of progress. For others it was the quintessence of evil. Organizations and political parties have flourished to promote planning. Others came into existence to oppose it. Not long after the end of World War II a sizable number of deeply concerned scholars from the United States and Western Europe gathered on a mountain top in Switzerland to form an organization devoted to international opposition to planning. It never developed any great influence, partly, I am told, because of an ideological schism over whether navies should be socially owned or privately provided on a lease-hire system by the private sector.

· 2 ·

In fact one can give a good deal of precision to the notion of planning. And as the meaning conveyed thereby has come to be better appreciated in recent times, much of the emotion has gone out of the discussion. In the modern and developed economy there is a certain choice as to how resources—labor, land, capital, natural resources—will be organized for productive purposes. The task, or a large part of it, can be entrusted to the market; this will interpret the wants of the consumer to the producer through the medium of higher prices and the promise of higher earnings. The market also sets in motion the investment of savings, the recruitment of labor, and the organization of the productive machinery which provides the needed and wanted products.

There is the alternative of a much more determinate organization of resources. Goals, specifying the things to be done and the goods to be produced, are proclaimed. The state then assumes the powers necessary to pursue these goals. In one way or another it ensures that the employment of labor and capital and the exploitation of other resources will contribute to, or be consistent with, the goals that have been specified. It establishes and operates the organizations that produce the goods.

The latter point is worth a further word. The theory of planning originated in close alliance with the theory of socialism—one of the reasons, more than incidentally, why the word "planning" was so long regarded in nonsocialist quarters with uneasiness. Socialist theory by its nature placed great emphasis on public ownership of natural resources and capital plant and, subject to political exigencies, of land. This was deemed necessary to prevent exploitation, ensure social justice, and ensure also that political power would not be arrogated by the owners of capital. With the development of the modern interest in planning, the public ownership and control of resources came almost implicitly to be considered both necessary and sufficient for ensuring a planned use of resources. With public ownership there could be planning; without public ownership there could be no effective planning.

In reality, as so often happens in the social sciences, we are dealing with distinctions that are far less sharp than the everyday discussion makes them out to be. Those countries that rely extensively on the market have, none the less, a substantial sector in which resources are organized by the state. If we take as the measure of the amount of planning the proportion of all current resources—gross national product—fully controlled and disposed of by the state, about 20 per cent of the American economy is planned. For India the comparable figure is 13–14 per cent. The market economy of the United States has a larger public sector than the socialist economy of India. And one could continue. While in the Soviet Union productive resources are fully owned by the state, considerable and skillful use is made of pecuniary incentives for labor and management. There is also a sizable market for privately produced agricultural products. In Poland as in Yugoslavia agriculture as a whole remains subject to market incentives.

A few weeks ago President Kennedy announced the first of a series of steps designed to carry a man to the moon. Along with most of my countrymen, and I think most men and women everywhere, I feel a sense of excitement over this adventure. But it is not a form of travel which will soon be put on a paying basis. The initial tickets will cost several billions of dollars apiece, a price which can be counted upon to discourage the average tourist. So this adventure cannot be left to the market; it can be the product only of planning. From the planned sector of the American economy also came atomic energy; from it also has come much modern electronic development. The modern jet air transport was similarly the product of planned development, a by-product of military procurement. Many of the other technical breakthroughs in the unplanned economies have had a similar origin in recent times. We have public initiative in planning without public ownership. The two are no longer indissolubly allied.

· 3 ·

I do not argue that the distinction between the planned and the unplanned economy is without meaning. But most of what the professional ideologists say about the distinction is without meaning. Many things must be planned even in those economic systems where the market has a major role. And the market plays an important part in the economic systems that are planned. We see a planned use of resources combined with public ownership of capital plant. We find it where the control and administration of capital remains in private hands. Clearly we must be wary of glib generalization in the discussion of planned and unplanned economies. I might add that there are few areas where it is more prevalent in our age.

What is not in doubt is the need for planning by the less developed country. For reasons I have just indicated there is much that the market can usefully encourage and accomplish. But the market cannot reach forward to take great strides when these are called for. As it cannot put a man in space so it cannot bring quickly into existence a steel industry where there was little or no steelmaking capacity before. Nor can it quickly create an integrated industrial plant. Above all, no one can be certain that it will do so in countries where development has lagged and where there is not only a need for development but an urgent demand that it occur promptly. To trust to the market is to take an unacceptable risk that nothing, or too little, will happen.

This is why in the developing country the word planning has ceased to be controversial. Five-year plans are the invention of, and were once the exclusive possession of, the Soviet Union. Now Americans and Western Europeans assemble without thought to consider how they may help finance the five-year plans of India or Pakistan. The country which does not have goals, and a program for reaching these goals, is commonly assumed to be going nowhere. This may well be so.

· 4 ·

Because planning is now taken for granted, we have been less critical of contemporary developments in its methods in recent years than would be desirable. In the last decade I have had occasion to examine a considerable number of these plans. And in the next world I face quite a few years in that well-populated part of purgatory where, it is known, economists are made to answer for all the advice they have given to governments. I am persuaded that it would be a grave error to imagine that the theory and practice of planning are completed edifices.

Earlier, I have stressed the need for accommodating our ideas of planning to the stage of development of the particular country. In the early stages of development, plan creation is not properly a matter of economic planning at all; rather it is to build basic administrative organs, to develop the educational and basic cultural structure, and to get a viable and progressive social system. In Western Europe and the United States these steps following the French and American revolutions laid the foundation for economic advance. In developing its Central Asian republics, as the visitor learns, the Soviets gave high priority to developing an effective system of provincial administration, to education, to providing a transportation system, and to getting the nomads into a settled system of agriculture. These steps were clearly regarded as prerequisites for further agricultural and industrial development.

It follows that in the early stages of development the task is not to set production targets and plan investment outlays. Rather it is to lay the administrative, social, and educational groundwork for such advance. Only in later stages is detailed planning of investment in order. This type of planning, that which is commonplace in India and Pakistan, belongs, relatively speaking, to a rather advanced stage of development. I should like now to comment on this planning.

· 5 ·

The standard modern development plan is an investment plan. It reflects decisions on how best to employ scarce capital resources. Its primary goal is the thing that investment is assumed to accomplish, namely, a specified and presumably adequate rate of economic growth. In this planning a good deal of thought goes into the matching and phasing of the various segments of the plan—into ensuring that kinds and amounts of steel being produced will match requirements for steel in kind and amount and that this balance between supply and requirements is maintained over time. Equally careful attention is accorded the supply of investment resources—the question of where, internally and externally, the capital is coming from. One can find little fault, in principle at least, with the way this part of the planning task is performed. There are, however, certain other things for which a good plan must provide, and the need for these is not always so clearly perceived. Let me mention the three further and often missing elements of a good plan.

First, a good plan must provide a strategy for economic advance. In the nature of a strategy some things are central—that is, strategic, clearly separate from that which is useful or passive. Among angels, it is known, virtue goes unnoticed. Likewise if everything is held to be vital the truly vital will escape attention. By way of illustration, in an industrialized country a highly efficient transportation system, a low-cost steel supply, and an economic and reliable source of power are all indispensable. With these something is certain to happen; without them one can be less sure. Certainly other aspects of industrialization, if not unimportant, are less important. Similarly in agriculture, while many things are useful, a few things are indispensable. Water, fertilizer, and improved seed can revolutionize agriculture. Most other agricultural services can work only moderate change.

Working against these strategic forces is the pressure of individuals, departments, and regions to have their favorite enterprises included in the modern plan. This pressure is great. The desire not to overlook anything is also strong. So the plan easily becomes not a plan but a list of all the things that everyone would like to have done or that anyone believes ought to be done.

Specification of the things of strategic urgency is lost.

In the American colonies prior to independence and in the early years of the Republic, there was no great surplus of food. The space between the mountains and the sea was limited and not everywhere fertile; the demands for food and fodder sometimes exceeded its capacity and food had to be imported from Europe. A plan formulated along modern lines for early American agriculture would have emphasized the need for agricultural colleges, extension services, veterinary services, plant breeding, better marketing, control of insect pests, and the provision of storage capacity for buffer stocks. Doubtless also there would have been mention of the need for improved transportation. But among the other excellent and useful ideas this could easily have been overlooked. In 1825 the State of New York opened a canal which connected the black lands of the West with the centers of population. On its completion the food shortage came to an end; there has, I am happy to say, been no sign of recurrence. This canal was the strategic factor in the plan. The importance of isolating and emphasizing the elements of strategic importance is not less in the developing country today.

· 6 ·

The second requirement of a good plan is that it emphasize both the visible and the invisible dimensions of industrial achievement. Like an iceberg, much of a modern industrial society is out of sight. And, also like an iceberg, it is its invisible part which has the greatest capacity for causing shipwreck. To get capital plant—steel mills, railway lines, coal mines, airplanes, oil rigs—into use is the visible achievement of development planning. To ensure that this plant is efficiently used—that management is independent and sound, that in consequence material costs are low, product quality good, cost-of-production low, and earnings adequate for replacement and expansion of plant—is the much larger part of the task. This part lies below the surface, and it is not sufficient that the developing country be only adequate in these respects. It must be more productive than its older competitors. It was by low cost and efficient production that Germany and Japan won their place in the industrial constellation against the competition of the earlier arrivals. New industrial countries such as Israel and Yugoslavia have recently been making their bid in the same way.

It is thus that earnings for further expansion, both domestic and foreign, are won.

I think it extremely important that the modern plan set firm targets for this invisible achievement. As valuable as firm targets for steel output are firm targets for man-hour productivity, costs, and returns. Goals so set become binding on all concerned. All are challenged to meet them. All have a sense of failure if there is a falling short in performance. And there is, in addition, the highly practical fact that failure can be identified with those responsible. If there are no standards then no one fails the examination. Promotion and honor accrue to all alike. Life was not meant to be that easy, and certainly not in a developing nation.

In much of our present planning we set targets for visible physical accomplishment—for capacity in place or for production. This is possibly the easiest and certainly the smallest part of the task. Targets are equally practical for managerial performance, labor productivity, costs, and returns; all lend themselves admirably to objective measurement. It is of the greatest importance that the modern development plan be as complete in respect of these goals as of any other.

· 7 ·

The final requirement of modern development planning is that it have a theory of consumption. As I have noted, much attention has
been given to the instruments for control of production. And much has been given to the means
for expanding productive capacity and achieving
an integrated and balanced growth. A theory of
consumption—a view of what the production is
ultimately for—has been surprisingly little dis-
cussed and has been too little missed. This is not
a subject which I have space to deal with extensively here. But let me suggest the nature of the
problem.

To say that production is planned is to say
that the market has in some measure been accepted as an authority on what should be produced. The decision has passed to government.

On what grounds should government decide?
How much should be withheld from present
consumption to nurture increased future consumption? If today's bread is barely sufficient,
can one ask for sacrifices therein so that tomor-
row's people will have butter?

More important, what kind of consumption
should be planned? Should it take the consump-

tion of the more highly developed countries as a model? Should it be guided by whatever market demand exists, which in most of the underdeveloped countries will reflect a considerable inequality of incomes, with the result that production will be heavily influenced by the wants of the well-to-do minority? Or should production be tailored above all to serving as cheaply as possible the recognizable needs and desires of the average low-income consumer?

If these questions are not faced deliberately they may be answered without thought. In particular there is danger that the consumption patterns of the more developed countries will be followed as a matter of course. Prestige—the wish to show off television and multilane highways—may play a part. The theory of consumption must be more democratic than this. Prime attention must be accorded goods that are within the range of the modal income—that can be purchased by the typical family. The burden of proof is strongly on the rest.

Cheap bicycles in a low-income country are thus more important than cheap automobiles. An inexpensive electric lighting system for the villages is better than a high-capacity system which runs equipment the people cannot afford. Inexpensive radio sets are important; television belongs to another day. Above all nothing is so important as abundant and efficiently produced food, clothing, and shelter, for these are the most universal of requirements.

India, I am glad to say, has gone farther than any other developing country in testing her consumer goods production against average need. But in all developing countries we need to have much more clearly in mind the particular consumer for whom in the last analysis the planning is done.

Specification of the strategically important, concern for the invisible as well as the visible requirements of industrial achievement, and a clear view of the consumer being served—these seem to me the unfinished business of modern development planning.

IV

Education and Economic
Development

IN these last years, as many new countries of
Asia and Africa have escaped colonial bond-
age and turned as first-class citizens to the tasks
of their national development, they have had to
decide what priority to accord to investment in
education. Should it have the very highest priority? Is education a prerequisite to all other
progress? Or should a certain economic base be
provided first? Only as increased production income is available does good education become
possible. Only from this will there be where-
withal to support schools and colleges and universities. Economic growth is necessary if a nation is to pay for schools and the teachers.

This has been the debate. It has been decided
in various ways. Sometimes, too, it has been de-

cided without anyone's seeing that there is an argument. Education has been given priority. Or other forms of expenditure—roads, airports, dams—have been put first because they seemed the first essential.

The problem of priority here is comparatively new. Uncertainty has entered with economics. Economic development in our day has come to be regarded overwhelmingly as a problem in economic analysis. In economic analysis, in turn, the role of education is ambiguous. This ambiguity has led to doubt and uncertainty as to what comes first.

· 2 ·

More specifically, we think of economic development as the investment of present resources for increased future production—the investment of savings for growth. We regularly measure the development effort of a country by the volume of its investment—what it saves from its own consumption, and what it is borrowing from consumers abroad, to invest in future increases in output. And here is the problem, for education is both a form of consumption and a kind of investment. Like bread, it is something we use or consume. But, like a dam or canal, it is something in which we invest to produce more in the future. This difference leads on to very different attitudes toward education in development. When we think of education as a consumer service, it becomes something on which we should save. Savings are necessary for investment, and savings are obtained by economizing on consumption. But when we think of education as an investment, it becomes something we should emphasize. We seek to expand investment. The resulting conflict in policy could scarcely be greater.

The contrasting attitudes which underlie this conflict are evident in almost every discussion of education. Convocation speakers the world around remind their highly indifferent audiences that man does not live by bread alone. The enrichment of the mind is as important as the nourishment of the body. Intellectual activity is properly pursued for its own sake; the poet, artist, or writer rightfully scorns economic gain as a test of performance. It was their tendency to apply economic calculation to refreshment of the spirit and mind which caused Carlyle to characterize economists as the learned professors of the dismal science. And who would say that people should be rescued from the serfdom of ignorance only in order to make them more productive? In these attitudes education is defended for its own sake—by my more vulgar definition, it is a consumer good. Though it is a rather superior consumer good, it has nothing directly to do with production. And those who take a less poetic view of matters righteously insist on the priority of ditches, dams, and fertilizer plants. For it is these that feed poets.

But there is another view. Studies by Theodore Schultz among others in the United States have recently shown that outlays for education may bring large increases in production. By the kind of calculation that Carlyle would have most abhorred, a dollar or a rupee invested in the intellectual improvement of human beings will often bring a greater increase in national income than a dollar or a rupee devoted to railways, dams, machine tools, or other tangible capital goods. To rescue farmers and workers from illiteracy may certainly be a goal in itself. But it is also a first indispensable step to any form of agricultural progress. Nowhere in the world is there an illiterate peasantry that is progressive. Nowhere is there a literate peasantry that is not. Education, so viewed, becomes a highly productive form of investment.

And this is true of many kinds of education. Most of us would agree on the importance of scientists and engineers for economic development. Machines are no more important than the men who make them, maintain them, or improve them. But the productivity of doctors and public health specialists is also very high. The suppression of malaria brings great increases in energy and output, as the experience of the last fifteen years has shown. (It also brings an astonishing output of babies, and, while we have talked of birth control in these last years, science has so far accomplished much more in promoting births than in preventing them.) The suppression of yaws and hookworm has a similar effect on productivity.

But not only scientists, engineers, and doctors are a good educational investment. There are surprising returns to esoteric and even exotic forms of knowledge. The linguist obviously maintains the avenues to the technology of other cultures. Literacy leads on to a demand for writers who can supply its market. And the accomplished writer adds to gross national production in precisely the same way as a successful farmer. Not even the artist, as an object of investment, may be ignored. One of the most suc-

cessful industries of modern India is motion
picture production. This industry flourishes only
in the presence of a secure artistic tradition in
the theater, music, ballet, and the visual arts. It
requires reasonably good artists to produce bad
pictures; it takes very good ones to produce good
pictures. No one ever invested in an artist with
a view toward helping the balance of payments.
Yet India's artistic tradition is serving admirably
to earn foreign exchange.

· 3 ·

The fact is that education is of high importance both as an object of immediate consumption and as a form of investment for future production. It is neither consumption nor investment, but both. To look at education as a form
of consumption, given the importance that the
developing country attaches to investment, is to
risk assigning it an unduly low priority. Some
new countries have almost certainly done so.
They have regarded their steel mills, dams, and
fertilizer factories as the tangible manifestation
of such development. Aswan, Volta, or Bhakra-
Nangal *are* development. They get the discussion, the money, the visitors, the glow of pride.
Well-trained teachers may provide a greater

promise of increased production. But they are not such tangible monuments to progress.

However, I have a feeling that this mistake is by way of being corrected—and I hasten to say that it has never been nearly so serious an error in India as in the less developed lands. India has held, on the whole, to the lesson of the nineteenth century, which is that education, or education abetted by honest and orderly government, comes first. I doubt, however, that any country has yet accepted all of the implications of education as a form of development investment. Neither university students nor faculties have yet seen the full significance of their claim as a form of investment on scarce development resources. Let me turn to this.

· 4 ·

If education, and henceforth I speak more specifically of university education, is regarded as a consumer service, we will naturally bring to it the attitudes that seemed appropriate to other forms of consumption. These include a high degree of permissiveness. The phrase "consumer sovereignty" is one of the oldest in economics; it implies the right of the consumer to choose between various forms of consumption. It implies, above all, to consume or not to consume, as he wishes.

This notion of consumer sovereignty, when brought to education, suggests that the student has the right to study or not to study as the consumer has the right to consume or not to consume. It implies that the choice lies with the inidvidual and the individual alone. It implies that his field of study is purely a matter of his own preference. No one may interfere with or guide his sovereign choice in these matters. But if, in fact, the student is the privileged object of the investment of scarce resources, the matter is not so clear. Society has given him some of its savings. Surely he has a clear obligation to return to society the increased production that society expects and for which it has spent its scarce substance. The more scarce the resources, the greater this obligation.

As I have noted, if education is viewed as a consumer good, it is the privilege of every individual to pursue the curriculum of his choice. Everyone has a right to an arts degree if that is the preferred and fashionable course of study. But if education is a form of investment, then planning of educational output becomes desirable and even imperative. Attention must be accorded to the distribution of talent between engineering, science, medicine, agriculture, and other needed specialties. I am not going so far as to suggest that students should be forced into a profession which they do not prefer. And the planning of university specialization is an exceedingly difficult matter. But I am certainly suggesting that when education is viewed as an investment, serious thought must be given to the accommodation of students to need and the incentives and other arrangements by which this is brought about.

· 5 ·

To view education as an investment will, I venture, have some bearing on university direction and administration. The university must be responsive to development requirements and it must be so organized as to make this possible. This means strong and responsive leadership by the faculty and its duly constituted representatives. The needs of the larger community must be effectively translated into curricula, courses, and good academic discipline. It is hard ever to take a stand against democracy. But the schoolmaster, at his best and in the most democratic countries, has always been a rather authoritarian figure. I doubt that a university can be wholly successful unless it reposes strong and responsible power in those who teach and unless those who teach delegate as needed to their own representatives. In recent times Latin American universities have been experimenting with highly democratic direction in which students, graduates, and faculty all participate more or less equally. Democratic or not, it is a formula for deterioration, incoherence, and chaos. I believe the university is by nature an oligarchy of its faculty. This is especially so if education is regarded purposefully as an investment from which the most of what is needed must be obtained.

· 6 ·

But I have no intention of allowing the faculty to escape without comment. It, too, has special responsibilities when education is viewed as a development outlay. By no means all of the traditional university practices and habits fit the requirements of the developing country. Thus, in most older university communities—mine is one—many faculty members have come to take a rather lofty view of teaching. We say that our primary task is research, or writing, or intellectual leadership. Students, we agree, are sufficiently privileged if they can see us passing in the street or listen thrice weekly to some uninspired and badly delivered lectures. These attitudes cannot be afforded if education is being tested by its productivity. Then the task of the teacher must be to mold and shape and guide and inspire his students to ensure that they are indeed a more productive property. If he fails to do so, he is squandering scarce public resources.

Nor can subject matter or degrees be copied as a matter of course by the university in the developing countries. As an economist, I look with considerable discontent on much of the economics that is taught in the new countries. It is not clinically concerned with the problems of these countries and pragmatically with their solutions. Rather it is often a fashionable elucidation of the sophisticated models and systems which are currently in fashion at Cambridge, the London School, or even at Harvard. As a layman I have sometimes wondered if medical education has been really adapted to the situation of the poor country. In the United States and Europe and, indeed, also in New Delhi, we yearn for doctors who are trained and totally trustworthy. The provision of such total training is the *sine qua non* of modern medical education. But in the developing country, with scarce resources, if we insist on these high standards for the few, may we not deny medical assistance to the many? Do we not get good doctors in the capitals at the price of having no one to set a broken leg or prescribe some morphine in the villages?

The problem of investment is always to obtain the kind of capital most appropriate to requirement at the lowest cost. There is indication in fields as diverse as medicine and economics that a less costly form of capital, better adjusted to the requirements of the developing country, could in fact be obtained. Investment, to speak technically, could be rationalized. No one would urge the wrong tractors for the underdeveloped country merely because they exist in America or the Soviet Union. So with education.

· 7 ·

But let me summarize and make a more general point. A developing country may rightfully regard its outlays for education as an investment. The fact that these have also the characteristics of consumption, and are rewarding to the individual in their own right, must not be allowed to confuse the issue. That something is both a consumer service and a source of productive capital for the society does not detract at all from its importance as an investment. Rather it enhances that importance.

But when we consider education as an investment, we must consider it as purposefully as any other form of capital outlay. This the older and more developed countries do not necessarily do or need to do. Their traditions are different; wealth has made it possible for them to be much more easygoing. The new country cannot be so permissive toward those in whom it invests. They are a privileged group who must work to deserve their privileges. The teachers are custodians of scarce national resources which must not be wasted. The country must be sure that its educational investment is adapted to its needs.

In short, the developing country must consider its educational system in the light of the peculiar requirements of development. It cannot simply adapt from the older models. Having come late to development, it is the good fortune of the new countries that they can learn from others. But it is their misfortune that so much of what exists in other countries cannot be copied without serious cost. Adaptation, as I have earlier suggested, is as demanding in its own way as innovation.

V

The Instrument of Production

I TURN now to the instrument of industrial
production in the developing country and,
in particular, to the institution which in some
form or other is essential for the conduct of
economic activity on any considerable scale. I
have reference to the corporation or company.

One must stress first of all the inevitability of
the corporate organization of production. The
world's religions are, on the whole, disappoint-
ingly unspecific on the nature of the economic
system in the hereafter. I have long wondered
why some economist hasn't asked the Ford
Foundation for a research grant to go into the
matter. We know that Heaven, as it is vouch-
safed to Christians, employs gold as a paving
material rather than as a medium of exchange
and that the principal consumer product is
a stringed instrument. We do not know the

nature of the production mechanism, whether for making harps or other goods. But even here we can be sure that if there is production of goods on any important scale it will be carried on by an industrial firm or corporation. In our inferior world certainly, whether in India, the United States, the United Kingdom, or the Soviet Union, where any productive task must be performed, the firm is ubiquitous and inescapable.

The reason is simple: modern productive activity—the making of steel, aluminum, fertilizer, lorries, or machine tools—requires a complex blending of skills and talents in a complex mosaic of tasks and functions. These skills and talents are not themselves rare, esoteric, or exceptional. If genius were required for economic activity our situation would be serious, for genius is always scarce and the supply highly unpredictable. The peculiar achievement of the industrial firm is that it combines the commonly available talent to do what the isolated individual could not possibly accomplish. It is a synthetic personality, in which many real personalities are combined, and its accomplishment is more than the sum of isolated individual contributions could ever be.

The corporate personality is not required for simple small-scale production such as most agriculture. It is not needed for most government functions—for the administration of justice, the collection of revenue, or the conduct of public education. These lend themselves to accomplishment within broad and stable rules. But the most characteristic feature of modern industry is the large scale of its units, the complexity of its technology, and the complex claims which the modern market makes upon it. Here there cannot be predetermined rules for every contingency. There must, instead, be adaptation to ever-changing circumstances, and the success of the adaptation will depend on the blending of varieties of technical knowledge and experience possessed by numerous individuals. This blending is accomplished by the corporation. For the conduct of complex tasks it is a competent and versatile, if synthetic or artificial, personality.

To see the corporation as a personality provides the prime clue to its administration. The individual or natural personality realizes itself only under conditions of liberty. To subject the behavior of one individual to the detailed surveillance of another is to ensure debasement and inferior performance. Individual achievement is at its best when the individual has a clear set of goals and the means, including of course the knowledge, with which to pursue these goals under the stimulus of his own will. As with the individual personality, so with the corporate personality. Autonomy, the independence to pursue specified goals, is equally important for the producing corporation. So are clearly specified goals. Indeed, these are more than important; they are the only administrative arrangement that is consistent with the effective corporate being.

· 2 ·

More specifically, the synthetic personality which we call the firm or corporation involves an intricate problem of cooperation and coordination among its parts. Much of this cooperation and coordination is accomplished automatically—it is the fruit of familiarity and confidence between the participants. One technician supplements his knowledge by resort to another —he knows to whom to turn and just how much confidence he can repose in the knowledge and judgment of the man whom he asks. The skilled worker similarly seeks help when his task takes him beyond the range of his own proficiency.

This also he does on his own volition. The manager must know when and how to help; but no single manager ever manages in the sense that he makes all the decisions. In the successful corporation, decision-making is deeply inherent in the corporate being.

There are equally numerous and intricate problems of coordination along the time dimension in the industrial firm. Modern industrial processes are closely interdependent; delay in one place will ordinarily cause delay with cumulative effect elsewhere. There is, accordingly, a high premium on timely decision. Perhaps the most distinctive requirement of the industrial establishment, as compared with the traditional government agency, is its dependence on timely decision. In the industrial firm a bad decision made on time will not usually be as costly as a good decision made too late. The bad decision can often be reversed at low cost. The time lost waiting for the good decision can never be retrieved.

The need for autonomy and the peculiar vulnerability of the corporation to outside influence are directly related to these characteristics. If external intervention affects people, it will impair or upset the complex and subtle set of relationships on which effective coordination depends. For example, the arbitrary withdrawal of a known and proven man and the substitution of another of unknown talent or reliability leads to immediate uncertainty as to how responsibility for decisions is to be shared, or the reliability of the decision in which the newcomer participates. Uncertainty and indecision result. A common form of external intervention is review of certain types of decisions—on procurement, product design, production techniques, prices, or the like. Inevitably this review takes time. Coordination on the time dimension suffers. In the process of preventing poor decisions, delayed and hence more costly decisions are ensured.

I must emphasize that the corporate personality is damaged by both well-intentioned and ill-intentioned intervention. There is little to choose between the two.

· 3 ·

In both modern American and modern Soviet organization there has been a large measure of accommodation to the requirements of the corporate personality for autonomy. The modern large American corporation enjoys almost complete independence from its stockholders, the principal source of external interference. While lip service is always paid to democratic control by the owners, it is recognized in practice that any extensive and effective interference by stockholders in management would be exceedingly damaging. (Suit is now pending against the principal owner of one of our large airlines to keep him from interfering with the management of the company he owns.) Thus all effective authority as regards production decision resides within the corporation. This authority is also jealously defended against the state.

I do not speak with equal confidence of economies of the Soviet type. But certainly no theme has received more emphasis in recent times than the need for according managers the independence and autonomy that enables them to do their job. Soviet factory managers, an impressively capable group of men, the visitor discovers, consistently stress the importance of such autonomy for the effective discharge of their responsibilities.

In the developing country, however, the autonomy of the corporate personality encounters a special challenge. In part this is because it will not have yet demonstrated the urgency of this protection to the corporate personality. But more particularly it is because choice and circumstance require that a good many operate in such countries under the direction of the state and in the democracies under the eye of parliamentary authority.

· 4 ·

The public enterprise in the parliamentary democracy is publicly owned for a purpose. One obvious purpose is the exercise of a measure of democratic control over the enterprise. This control ensures that the firm's procedures and decisions will be in the public interest—that its decisions are sound and sensible and serve the general good. If there is no effort to exercise this control, some at best will say there is no purpose in public ownership. But plausible and innocent though this sounds, especially when we interject the magic phrase "democratic control" into the discussion, we have here a serious and often unsuspected contradiction. If individuals within the corporate organization are servants of a force outside the organization, they will no longer think automatically of the goals of the organization. They have, at best, a dual obligation: one part of the obligation runs to the firm and the other to the external authority. One eye is on the organization; the other is on the parliament or other public authority. The multitude of decisions will not automatically be attuned to the needs of the corporation. In short, the dual obligation is inconsistent with the requirements of the corporate personality, which calls for the implicit commitment of many people to the common goal.

The external authority has an even more damaging effect on the time dimension of decision-making. I have stressed the importance of timeliness as compared with precision in industrial decisions. But the man who must answer to a parliamentary committee or brief a minister will always reserve to himself the right to review the decisions that he must later defend. Moreover, executive departments and parliaments are ordinarily concerned not with late decision but with wrong decision. It is on these that a man can score his points. The result is centralized and hence delayed decision. And they mean the waste that goes with delay. These are damaging to the corporate personality, which should distribute decision-making authority on the level where it can be exercised with the optimal combination of accuracy and expedition. Even if slow decisions are criticized they will not be easily corrected. The need to protect against the wrong as compared with the untimely decision, even though the latter may be intrinsically the more damaging, will remain.

The problem, I repeat, is not of wisely motivated or of ill-motivated intervention. Rather it is of anything that interferes with or distorts and destroys the firm or corporate personality. This is a matter of the utmost importance, for external influence with its impairment of autonomy will always defend itself on the grounds of the wisdom or sincerity of its motivation. This is not a defense.

· 5 ·

I have noted that the corporate body, like the individual, is effective only if it has liberty to pursue specified goals. This allows the full development of its personality. The second great problem of the public corporation in the parliamentary democracy concerns the goals. Paradoxically, while there is grave danger that parliamentary or other public authority will circumscribe the decision-making process and hence impair the personality of the firm, there is also danger that it will not be sufficiently aggressive and firm in specifying goals. Hence the standards of achievement of the publicly owned firm will be insufficiently clear.

The goals of the modern industrial corporation in the United States or Western Europe are reasonably specific: broadly speaking, the most successful corporation is the one that makes a good profit and achieves a rate of growth greater than its rivals. (To be head of a profitable organization is an undoubted source of esteem in the United States, but higher honors are invariably accorded to the sizable firm which can claim a greater rate of expansion.) The setting of targets for production and profit, and the drive to meet and exceed these goals, is a classic feature of Soviet planning.

The goals of the public corporation in the developing country have rarely been so clear. To maximize profits seems suspiciously like old-fashioned capitalism, which many of the new countries reject. The obligation to grow and expand has rarely been definite and firm. Subjective goals, such as the rendering of good service to the community or concern for workers, have been common. They have the handicap of their subjectivity—it is open to anyone to contend whether they are or are not being met. Those responsible often find it personally advantageous

to spend more time asserting their good performance than in ensuring it.

· 6 ·

You will not be in any doubt as to how I see
the solution. The industrial firm, by one designa-
tion or another, is inevitable for industrial development. It has a demanding personality; the
major demand is an autonomy in everyday
decision-making that is nearly absolute. That
autonomy extends to the right to make mistakes,
for error will often be the price, and a small one,
for expedition. The need for autonomy in the
conduct of military operations is equally great. It
is accorded as a matter of course. Nor can it be
denied that generals have exercised to the full
their privilege of making mistakes. In military
theory the delay that excludes error is the one
unforgivable mistake. In the United States a
few years ago one of our large automobile com-
panies produced an automobile which was a
serious error. Great outlays were made on the
theory that the public wanted a very large
vehicle with something of the physiognomy of a
surprised frog. The public was not at all inter-
ested. Had this been a publicly owned corporation
the criticism would have been acute. Doubtless

it would have led to the requirement that all changes in car design should henceforth be submitted to a panel of public reviewers. The result might have been the avoidance of similar mistakes. One imagines that another result would have been recurrent and in the end much more costly delays while the panel resolved the problems of automobile aesthetics. The need for this autonomy is not peculiar to our system or any system. It is required by the nature of the corporation in all systems.

Autonomy must include, subject only to standards designed to prevent abuse, hiring and firing of personnel. It is flexibility here that makes possible the complementing of one skill by another, one man's knowledge with that of another, and which enables the synthetic personality which we call the firm to do what no individual can do. The intrusion of politics and patronage into the public corporation is deeply subversive of the subtle relationships on which an effective development of this synthetic personality depends. But so also will be the intrusion of civil service procedures and routines. The latter may be admirably designed to ensure equality of treatment for all employees. But the effect can be to destroy the easy interpersonal adjustments and the automatic coordination on which effective operation depends. The world is full of unhappy choices, and in modern industrialism one of them is between perfectly just rules and reasonably satisfactory performance.

· 7 ·

But if the corporation must be protected in its personality from intrusion by outside authority upon its decisions, outside authority must be unremittingly firm in what it asks of the corporation. The goals it sets must be clear and utterly explicit. Success in all societies is in large measure its own reward, but there must never be any doubt as to what success consists of.

If I had to lay down a measure for performance for the publicly owned corporation in the developing country it would be the earnings that it provides to put into its own expansion. Such expansion, in the given or related field and within the framework of plan, would be considered the prime goal of the public-sector firm. The most successful firm would be the one which by its efficiency and drive finds the earnings that allow it the greatest growth. Perhaps there are other goals that may be urged. But what is vital is that the goal, whatever it is, be specific, measurable, known to all, and firmly enforced.

Though the society should be wholly tolerant

of errors that are within the framework of success, it should be wholly intolerant of failure to achieve the specified goals. Indeed, the non-achievement of goals, not the individual mistake, is the meaning of failure. Autonomy does not mean less public accountability. On the contrary, it means more. But it is accountability not for method, procedure, or individual action but for result.

Index